THE PINNACLE OF COMPASSION

Ten Ways We Can Be More Like Jesus

James Taiwo

INTRODUCTION

The life of Jesus on Earth was a life of compassion. He lived it and breathed it; therefore, it is not surprising that the bible is full of stories associate Jesus with compassion. It took a great deal of compassion for him to leave his throne in blissful heaven to suffer and die for mankind. We were drowning in the mire of sin, and Jesus came to save us because he was full of compassion. Romans 5:8 tells us that Jesus came to die for us while we were yet sinners and completely unworthy of this great gift. If we were worthy, we would have understood his reasons but, despite of our unworthiness, he still came. This took great compassion, because he saw that we were headed for destruction, and he did not want that to happen. When Jesus came to Earth, he further demonstrated compassion through his stories and in the way he lived. He led an exemplary life, largely for the sake of his disciples and those who believed in Him, so they could see how He handled issues and do the same. Today, Christ expects us to read the stories that He told and learn about how He lived His life so that we can follow his example. Christ will only be pleased with us when He sees us living as He has showed us. The succeeding chapters have, therefore, been written for us to see Christ in His moment and make Him our special example. It is easier to emulate what has been illustrated for us, and that is the purpose of this book. I have picked different stories from the Bible that illustrate compassion, that either Jesus told as parables or are about how He related with the people of His time. Also, to elucidate their meaning, I have included possible questions that might spring up from these stories, as well as providing answers for each. Read with your family and friends and talk about ways in which we can all be more compassionate as we follow Jesus' example.

Chapter One

THE GOOD SAMARITAN

Text: Luke 10:30-37

Main Story

In the bible story that appears before the story of the Good Samaritan, an expert of the law came to ask Jesus what the greatest law was, and Jesus told him, "Loving the Lord, our God" and that the second greatest is loving our neighbor as ourselves. The man wanted to test Jesus, and he asked: "Who is my neighbor." Luke 10:29 (NKJV).

Jesus, therefore, answered him with the parable of the Good Samaritan. In the story, a man was on a journey when he was attacked by bandits, who took everything he had and beat him badly. While he was lying there on the side of the road, a passing priest saw the man. Instead of helping him, he deliberately crossed to the other side of the road and kept on walking.

A Levite also passed by but, just like the priest, instead of helping, he crossed to the other side and went on his way.

Then a Samaritan came, saw the man and felt compassion for him. He stopped, despite the fact that the wounded man was Jewish (Samaritans and Jews typically did not relate with one another because the Jews saw the Samaritans as impure Israelites).

The Samaritan tended to the man's wounds and took him on his donkey to an inn, where he treated him further. The next day, he gave some money to the innkeeper to continue his care. The Samaritan also told the innkeeper that if he had cause to spend more, he would give him the money the next day.

Jesus ended the story by asking the expert of the law, "Who among the three acted like a neighbor?" The man said the one that showed mercy. Jesus told him to go and do the same.

Story Analysis

When we read this story, we can see that Jesus deliberately used a Jewish man and a Samaritan, because he wanted us to understand that he does not discriminate against anybody. His arms are open to everyone.. The Jews and Samaritans usually stayed away from one another, their relationship contentious, much like those between the different ethnic groups of today. Normally, it was considered a strange thing— even taboo—for a Jew to be found talking to a Samaritan. That is why the woman by the well in John 4 was surprised when Jesus asked her for water, considering she was a Samaritan and Jesus was a Jew. But Jesus was trying to teach her that, in the eyes of God, there is no discrimination or separation.

Also, we can see clearly that compassion does not always reside in the breast of a leader in the church. The priest and Levites were both titled and recognized people in the temple, but they had no compassion. One might expect that these people, who are basically the moral leaders of the Jews, would act correctly; this is an important part of the story's lesson. Being a priest of a man or woman of God does not automatically make a person like God. Our leaders in the church are just as susceptible to sin as any other human, and often they think better of themselves than they should. Jesus was the greatest leader the church has ever known, and he never held himself above others.. The priest and Levite could not act as God expected them to; they felt they were superior to the Jewish man lying in the gutter. It is up to each of us to make sure our attitude pleases the Lord and that our leaders are doing the right thing before we follow their example.

The help that the injured man got came from nowhere. He never would have expected that the Samaritan man, who was not expected naturally to associate with him, would have been the one to save him. But life does not work in black and white and sometimes, help comes from where we least expect it to. Sometimes, the people we look down on the most are those that would be there to help us in our hour of need.

The Samaritan man went all the way with his help. He did not take the man to the inn and leave him hanging. He made sure he was completely all right before he left. He even offered to pay more if the money he had given the innkeeper was not enough.

The major point we gain from this story is that the person least expected to show compassion was the one who was compassionate. The others, who were well-versed in the law and the prophets, were expected to know what to do, but they all turned their backs on the pain of the wounded man.

Take-Home Lessons

Jesus was letting us know that no matter the person, we are expected to show mercy. There should be no discrimination against people because of their ethnicity, status in the church, or gender, and we should make *everybody* feel accepted. Whoever it is that needs our help should be helped, and we should not base our compassion and help on whether the person is of the same religion, gender, ethnic group or race as us.

Compassion is not automatic, so it is a quality we can and should cultivate. The fact that you are a leader in the church or you have a position in your fellowship does not mean you are automatically compassionate. Every trait that Jesus expects us to have is not necessarily inherent simply because we have a position in the religious hierarchy. We have to pray for God's grace to be compassionate if we find we are lacking in it.

One who is compassionate will always have God's approval. God is compassionate; that is why he blesses us even when we do not deserve it. He expects us to treat others with the same compassion and consideration. Jesus told this story to show his approval of the man who was compassionate among all. If we want heaven to speak kindly of us and with approval, then we need to be compassionate.

It's not good enough to be halfway compassionate; you have to go all the way for it to count. The Samaritan made sure he did all he could for the man to be completely healed. We need to learn from this. We cannot leave people half-healed and say we have shown compassion. No—being truly compassionate means you are *all in*.

Questions to Contemplate

1. Why did Jesus have to tell the story of the Good Samaritan when the people asked him who their neighbor was?
2. Why did Jesus use a Samaritan and not another Jew?

$\mathcal{A}$pplication Answers

1. If we look at the life of Jesus, we can see that he told a lot of stories to make some concepts easier for people to understand. Naturally, humans are more receptive to listening attentively when a lesson comes wrapped in a good story. Jesus knew that the lessons would seem more real to them if he gave real-life examples. Truthfully, he easily could have answered them when they asked him about their neighbor, but he chose to tell them a story that would make the lessons resonate with them.

2. Jesus used a Samaritan so the people could see that your neighbor is not necessarily the one who is of the same gender, class, ethnicity or race. Your neighbor is any human being that was created by God. As humans, we are likely to consider the people who we feel have something in common with us as our neighbors and those in need of our help. But through this parable, Jesus has made it clear to us that *all* peoples are our neighbors and should be given equal consideration. One should not reject or discriminate against a person simply because he does not celebrate your faith beliefs. *All* are worthy of compassion.

Chapter Two

THE PARABLE OF THE UNFORGIVING DEBTOR

Text: Matthew 18:21-35

Main Story

In the parable of the unforgiving debtor, Jesus was teaching his disciples the need to forgive one another of wrongs. Peter asked Jesus how many times he should forgive a wrong done to him, and Jesus told him seventy times seven times. Then, to underscore his point, he told them a story. In the parable, a certain king was checking his records to settle accounts with his servant. A servant was, therefore, brought to him who owed him ten thousand talents. The king ordered that since the servant could not pay back the debt, the servant and his family, as well as all his belongings, would be sold to pay the debt.

The servant fell face down before the king and pleaded for mercy, asking the king to give him more time to pay the debt. The king was moved with compassion when he saw this and decided to let the servant go. He forgave him the debt and released him.

As this servant left the palace, he saw another servant who owed him 100 denarii. He grabbed that servant by the throat and asked him to pay him the money he owed. This fellow servant pleaded for mercy, also asking for time to pay when he had the money. This servant, who had just been forgiven his own debt, did not listen. He threw his fellow servant into prison till he was able to pay back the debt.

Other servants, who knew how kind their master had been to this unforgiving man, were grieved that he could throw his fellow servant into prison for debt when he himself had just been forgiven . They went and told the king.

The king sent for this servant and with anger said to him, "You wicked servant! I forgave you all that debt because you begged me. Should you not also have had compassion on your fellow servant, just as I had pity on you?" Matt 18:32-33 (NKJV).

The master, then, delivered him into the hands of torturers, sentenced to stay in the prison until he could pay back his debt.

Jesus concluded by saying that, "So my heavenly father also will do to you if each of you, from his heart, does not forgive his brother his trespasses." Matthew 18:35.

Story Analysis

There is always a time for accounting. The master in this story can be likened to God and, just as he brought in his books to make his accounts, God also has time when he sits to make account of all his people and how they have been living their lives.

The master, who was owed much, was ready to forgive. Imagine if you owed a debt of about 100 million dollars and you were forgiven that debt without needing to make any kind of payment or meeting any kind of condition. It is really amazing how compassionate a heart the master had. The master knew that the servant could not have found anywhere near the amount of money he owed, but still the master was willing to let it all go. That is how amazing our God is. No matter how deep the debt of our sin, God in his compassion is willing to forgive us. The story was told to teach the disciples forgiveness.

Jesus told the story in answer to his disciples asking how many times they were expected to forgive one another for repeated offenses. It is obvious from the story that one cannot forgive without compassion. It is compassion for a person's situation that moves us to forgive their wrongs against us. When we have pity on them and don't want them to keep wallowing in the guilt of what they have done, we forgive.

The unforgiving servant does not have compassion, and he also does not think of God's goodness. If he was compassionate and remembered the goodness done to him, he wouldn't have thrown his fellow servant in prison. The amount the king forgave him for was millions, but he could not forgive a hundred. Clearly, it is not the weight of the offense that sometimes determines why people are unforgiving; it is the lack of compassion. The one who had the bigger offense to forgive was the master, and he forgave easily.

There are consequences for being unforgiving. The servant enjoyed forgiveness until he displayed a lack of forgiveness and the king's pardon was withdrawn. If we lack compassion toward others enough to forgive them, then we are preparing ourselves for a lack of forgiveness from God.

Take-Home Lessons

1. We have learned that compassion is what moves the heart to have pity on others and set them free from whatever we have against them. A heart that is not compassionate is unforgiving. We, therefore, need to learn to be compassionate so we can forgive others for the wrongs that have been done to us. When we think about how sad they must feel being in that web of being unforgiven, a compassionate heart is what we need to set them free.

2. God is ever-ready to forgive us. He is full of compassion. Let us not feed into the lies the devil tells. Anytime we err against

God, instead of trying to run away from him, we should go to him, pleading for mercy, and he will forgive us.

3. If you don't forgive, you will not be forgiven. It's simple. God expects us to forgive others if we want to keep enjoying his forgiveness. Also, so we can reign with him on the last day, we need to forgive others of their wrongs toward us.

Questions to Contemplate

1. Why did Jesus use money and debt instead of normal everyday offenses?
2. What was the account that was spoken of in this parable?

Application Answers

1. Jesus had to use money because he knew that the love of money was one of the greatest temptations of man. His disciples were asking him about how many times they were supposed to forgive others of their offenses. From their questions, it was clear that they were expecting Jesus to agree that if a particular person's offenses reached a certain peak, then you are allowed to not forgive. However, Jesus wanted to show them that no matter how grievous their offenses, we have no reason not to forgive others. He used the very thing he knew people would have issues with to drive home his point. He made us understand that there is no offense that others can perpetrate that is bigger than our sin, the sin that God not only forgave but sent his son to die for. It might seem impossible to forgive some people. What if someone hurts your child? How do you forgive him?

Harboring anger and despair in your heart will keep you from healing. If God can do it, then we surely can. He has given us the strength to do so.

2. The accounting spoken about in this parable is the account God makes of the sins that we are likely to commit in this lifetime that we are supposed to pay for. The sin is the great debt that the servant (who represents us) owes. And it is that same huge debt of sin that God is willing to wipe out completely from our records through the death of Christ. He, therefore, expects that having done us so great a favor, we will repay it by also forgiving our fellow humans for their wrongs.

Chapter Three

THE PRODIGAL SON

Text: Luke 15:11-31

Main Story

Jesus told the story of two brothers to explain our relationship with our father, God. In the parable, a rich man had two sons. One day, the younger son told the father to give him his share of his father's property. The father gave the son his share. A few days later, the son gathered together all his father had given him and journeyed to a far-off country. When he got to there, he squandered the riches.

After he had spent his inheritance, there was a famine in the land and he began to be in serious need. When he lacked food, he went to a man of the far-off place, who sent him to work among his swine. He was so hungry that the pods he fed the swine with looked good to eat.

One day, he came to his senses finally and said to himself, "At home, even the hired servants have food enough to spare, and here I am dying of hunger! I will go home to my father and say, "Father, I have sinned against both heaven and you, and I am no longer worthy of being called your son. Please take me on as a hired servant" Luke 15:17-19 (NLT).

Having made this decision, he returned to his father. While he was still a long way off, his father saw him coming. Filled with love and compassion, his father ran to meet him. When his father got to him, he quickly recounted all the things he had planned to say to his father. He told his father how he was no longer worthy to be called his son and was ready to be a servant.

But his father was so excited to see him, he did not listen to all the son was saying. Instead, he quickly summoned his servants to bring the finest robe in the house and put it on him and also get a ring for his finger and sandals for his feet. The father also asked that a fatted calf be killed to celebrate with a feast, for he said, "This son of mine was dead and has now returned to life. He was lost, but now he is found" Luke 15:24 (NLT).

Everything was done according to the father's request, and a feast began in honor of the son. When the older son returned from the fields where he had been working, he heard noise from the house and asked of one of the servants what was happening. The servant told him they were celebrating his brother's return.

The older brother became angry, and he refused to enter the house. His father came outside to meet him, to plead with him to come inside. But the son told his father that he has been a faithful son, and his father has never given him even so much as one young goat to go celebrate with his friends. When the prodigal son came back, however, his father celebrated him with richness.

His father told him, "Look, dear son, you have always stayed by me, and everything I have is yours. We had to celebrate this happy day. For your brother was dead and has come back to life! He was lost, but now he is found!" Luke 15:32 (NLT).

. . .

Story Analysis

The younger son came to his senses, realized that he had erred, and went to his father to ask for forgiveness. He didn't wait when he realized his mistake; he did not allow the devil to keep him tied down with guilt. And he also went ready to humble himself to his father. He knew what he had done required groveling and being humble, and he was ready to take the place of a servant just to get back in his father's good graces.

The father was compassionate; that is why he was able to forgive his son for so big a transgression. It is amazing how the father did not even bother to question the son but was just so excited to have him back. When we read the story, we notice that the father ran to meet the son while the son was still a distance away. It seems that even before the son came home, the father was watching out for his arrival. It takes a heart that is longing to even recognize from afar someone that has been gone so long. It just shows how much God is different from us; we probably would have forgiven, but we would have done it after many pleas and maybe even made the son prove himself. This father was not even interested in the pleas; the fact that his son was back was enough for him.

The older brother was not compassionate and was thinking only about himself, so much so that he forgot that the possessions of his father belonged to him as well as to his brother. All he had to do was ask his father if he needed a young goat to celebrate with his friends, but he didn't, and he felt bad that his father forgave his brother. He probably would have felt better if his father had meted out punishment on his son instead.

Take-Home Lessons

1. God expects us to show compassion to the people

around us the way that the father showed compassion to his son. Some of us are so vengeful that we believe in getting our own pound of flesh, but we did not learn that from our savior. He regarded people with compassion and forgave them their offenses; we should do the same.

2. We should learn the lesson from the prodigal son of going to God in humility and with a contrite heart when we sin against him. We cannot afford to take God's kind heart for granted. While we know that he will always forgive us, because that is his nature, we should not take his forgiveness for granted and become proud before him. Anytime we do something wrong, we should not run away from God but go to Him for forgiveness; however, we should go with humility. Some people think, "Well, if God will always forgive me, I can go around sinning all I want and then at the last minute ask for forgiveness." When we humble ourselves before God, it needs to be sincere. If we are thinking in our hearts that we will just go out and do the same thing again because we can be forgiven again, we are not being true to ourselves or God. We have to beg forgiveness with the true intent to sin no more.

3. Some of us have the tendency to be envious when others are shown compassion. As believers, we should not only show compassion but also support it in any way we can. We should not be like the brother, who was not happy about the father forgiving the other son. When we hear about forgiveness, it should fill us with joy. In fact, we should be among those preaching about forgiveness, and not discouraging others from forgiving. Have you ever heard someone say, "How can you let him get away with that!? He should be punished!" Leave the punishment to God and forgive.

*Q*uestions to Contemplate

1. Who do the people in the parable represent in our everyday lives?
2. Why did the father give the son the properties he asked for, and why did no one go after the son?

$\mathcal{A}$pplication Answers

1. The father in the story is God, who loves us all unconditionally, whether we are at our best or not. The two sons are us, humans, who belong to the father because he created us all. The prodigal son depicts those who now have wandered away and decided to live their own lives outside of God. The older son depicts Christians who are still with God, who feel all he owns belong to them as well. However, the older son had the self-righteous attitude that we, as Christians, so often display. We, who have been saved by grace, always find it hard to extend the same grace to people around us. God wants us to be gracious to others as he is gracious to us.

2. Truly, when we consider what happened here in the context of our earthly fathers, we can see that while they might not be able to stop you from leaving the house, especially if you are grown, they will likely not give you any property. Our earthly fathers will remind you that it is theirs and you have no right to demand it. But we are not dealing with man, we are dealing with God, and God does not act like man does. God is not task-master who is interested in robots. He is the one that created us; he could make us act exactly like he wants us to, but he wants us to have free will. God wants us to have the choice to be with him or not, so if we ever say we do not want to be with him, he lets us

go. Not because he does not love us, because in our absence, he will long for our return like the father of the prodigal son. Still, he will respect our choice, and he will always rejoice should we choose to return.

Chapter Four

THE FEEDING OF THE FOUR THOUSAND

Text: Matthew 15:32-39, Mark 8:1-9

Main Story

Jesus was teaching by the Sea of Galilee, and there was a multitude of people there who were interested in hearing him speak, and the multitude of people was growing. He called to his disciples and told them he had compassion for the multitudes because they had been with him for three days without food to eat and, if he sent them back home hungry, some of them would likely faint on the way, especially as some of them came from a long distance.

The disciples wondered how Jesus was planning on feeding them all. They voiced their concerns and asked him how they were supposed to find food for the multitudes in the desert.

Jesus then asked them how many loaves of bread they had. They told him they had seven. They also found few fishes. Jesus asked his disciples to get the people to sit down on the grass in groups.

When the people were seated, Jesus took the loaves, thanked God and broke them into pieces; then he asked his disciples to distribute them among the people.

Everybody ate as much as they wanted and were filled. When

they were done, the disciples were able to gather seven large baskets of leftovers. And Jesus sent them home.

They were about four thousand that Jesus fed that day, with only seven loaves and few small fishes.

Story Analysis

The crowd of people that followed Jesus was not summoned to Jesus to hear him speak. They came of their own free will to hear him, because they discovered he spoke words of truth and life. If you gathered people for an event for three days, you would be in big trouble if you didn't provide food, but if they came to meet you on their own, then you are not responsible, and neither was not Jesus. This wasn't a time-share seminar where attendees are fed because the folks running the show want to sell condos. However, because of his compassion, Jesus wasn't about to let the crowd go hungry. He felt their pangs of hungers as though they were his own. He felt compassion even though he was not the one who gathered them. He didn't ask them to pay for the food, either.

The compassionate heart of Jesus moved him to be proactive. These people did not complain to Jesus that they were hungry, but he knew they were because he could see they had not eaten for three days. Jesus could envision that some of them were likely to faint on the way if he sent them home without food. He paid attention to details, knowing some of them came from a distance.

Blessings follow a compassionate heart. Being compassionate means helping other people, and that is a quality that touches the heart of God. Jesus was compassionate, and they were able not only to feed thousands, but they had leftovers. They probably would not have been so blessed if everybody had been left to fend for themselves.

· · ·

ake-Home Lessons

1. This story shows how compassionate Jesus is. We are expected as Christians to feel the pain of others. We should not just be sympathetic; we should be empathetic. It is important that we act like Jesus and put ourselves in the shoes of others. There is a difference between recognizing the pain of others and actually being moved to action. The compassion of Jesus is not a passive; it is an active emotion that makes sure its object is helped. It is the type of compassion Jesus expects us to imbue as well.

2. A compassionate person is proactive. We should take our cue from Jesus. If we do not put ourselves in the shoes of others, we cannot pay attention to details enough to see where people are hurting and how badly they can hurt. The only way we can be compassionate enough to help in the right way is if we see, feel and understand their pain. We cannot afford to be nonchalant about others as Christians, because that is not what we learned from our Lord and Savior.

3. In the same vein, if we lead with compassion, we can be sure that it will not go unrewarded. Just like the crowd was left with extra baskets, we would also have multiple blessings by being compassionate.

uestions to Contemplate

1. Why did Jesus give thanks before breaking the bread?
2. Who took the leftovers home?

*𝒶*pplication Answers

1. Jesus gave thanks because he knew in advance that his father would multiply the meal. This is basically an example of how we should do what we are told to do, especially by God, in all circumstances, because he always shows up at the right time. A lot of us find it hard to thank God in advance for what we have yet to see, but Jesus is showing us an example here that it is possible. Jesus was also thanking God for all his father had done earlier for him. Even if we cannot thank God for what he is yet to do, at least we should be grateful for that which he has done before we came to him with different kinds of requests.

2. It is not written in the Bible who took the leftovers home; we should not bother ourselves about that. The main point of the story is clear. Jesus was compassionate enough to consider how the people who had been with him for three days were going to eat and he made do with the little food that was available to them. A miracle happened.

Chapter Five

THE FEEDING OF THE FIVE THOUSAND

Text: Matthew 13:14-21, Mark 6:30-44, Luke 9:10-27, John 6:5-14

Main Story

Jesus sent his disciples to preach the gospel and to heal the sick. When they came back and told them everything they had done, he took them privately toward a town called Bethsaida. The people still found out about it and followed them, and they were a large crowd. They looked like sheep without shepherd, so Jesus had compassion for them and began to teach them. He also healed them.

At the end of the day, the disciples came to Jesus and told him to send the people away to go into the surrounding villages and towns to get food for themselves. Instead, Jesus told them to get food for the people to eat. They asked him if they should buy two hundred pennyworth of food for the multitude, because they were about five thousand men without counting the women and children. Jesus asked them how many loaves they had. The disciples found out that a little boy had five loaves of bread and two fishes, and they reported this to Jesus.

Jesus asked them to ask the people to sit in groups of fifties and hundreds. He took the five loaves of bread and two fishes, blessed them and gave them to the disciples to distribute among the people. The people ate and they were all filled.

Afterward, the disciples were able to get twelve baskets of leftovers.

Story Analysis

Jesus wanted to have a quiet time alone with his disciples. He was not expecting the crowd to find out and follow them. But when they came, He did not send them away. He had compassion for them and taught them as well as healing their sick. Jesus did not mind that His schedule was tampered with. As far as Jesus is concerned, every time is a time to help, even if it went contrary to his plans. Helping with compassion was his priority.

The disciples were ready to send the people away to fend for themselves. But Jesus, out of his compassionate heart, wanted to give the people food. He did not consider sending the people away but rather seeing to their physical needs after he had satisfied their spiritual needs. Jesus understood that meeting people's spiritual needs would only be possible when their physical needs were met. People who are dead or faint out of starvation cannot hear the gospel and, if they are hungry, they cannot concentrate enough to hear of God's goodness.

The little boy, who was ready to share his food, must have been a very generous person. Imagine if he decided he did not want to give his food away, they would have had to look for a meal somewhere else. But he did not mind sharing what he had with others. The little boy must have had a heart of gold.

Take-Home Lessons

1. A compassionate person has to be selfless. There are times when we would want to put ourselves before others, but we cannot afford to do that as Christians. As Christians, God expects us to put him first and others next before

ourselves. Jesus was always selfless and exhibited traits of self-sacrifice, and we must follow his example.

2. As Christians, we cannot act like the disciples, but we have to act like Jesus, who is our perfect standard. We should always consider others in our decisions. We should not be like the disciples, who were ready to send the people away with empty stomachs without a care in the world about what they would eat.

3. It is unheard of for a Christian to be stingy; we have to be generous like the little boy. Christians cannot be found hoarding things but be ready to share with others. People who are not generous cannot call themselves Christians. We should be an example everywhere to unbelievers, so they can know the kind of person our Jesus is. When we are compassionate enough to share what we have, no matter how little, we find that we have enough for all through God's grace. If you are in a situation where you only have one slice of ham and five people, cut it up five ways. If you see someone on the street who is hungry and you have a sandwich, give him half. Don't worry about whether he is a scammer or genuinely in need. God will take care of the rest.

Q uestions to Contemplate

1. Why did Jesus ask his disciples to feed the people?
2. Who took the leftovers?

$\mathcal{A}$ pplication Answers

1. Jesus was trying to test his disciples and, as we can see from the passage, they failed woefully. Jesus knew what

he was going to do. He knew he could get food if he wanted to—after all, he is the son of God and he is God. But he wanted to see if his disciples had learned anything since they had been with him. They should have at least known that Jesus would never leave hungry people to starve, and they also should have known that Jesus, who had done numerous miracles before them, could feed a multitude without issue.

2. Just like the feeding of the four thousand, it is not clear who took the leftovers home. Many have, however, speculated that it could have been the little boy who took the leftovers home; after all, the initial five loaves and two fishes were his. It's possible. We cannot say, though, so we should not speculate on matters that we know not of. Like the feeding of the four thousand, we saw the compassion of Jesus displayed here, and the generosity of a little boy, who was ready to share his meal with others.

Chapter Six

THE ADULTEROUS WOMAN

Text: John 8:1-11

Main Story

Jesus was at the temple very early one morning when the Jewish leaders decided to test his sense of judgment. He was seated at the temple and a crowd soon gathered. As usual, Jesus taught them. While he was teaching the people, the teachers of religious law and the Pharisees brought forth a woman who had been caught in adultery. They placed her in front of the crowd.

They said to Jesus, "Teacher, this woman was caught in the act of adultery. The Law of Moses says to stone her. What do you say?" John 8:4-5 (NLT).

They were trying to trap him into saying something they could use against him, perhaps to prove he was not who he proclaimed to be. But, instead of saying anything, he stooped low and wrote in the dust with his finger.

When they saw he had yet to say anything, they kept demanding an answer from him. Jesus then raised his head up and said to them, "All right, but let the one who has never sinned throw the first stone!" John 8:7 (NLT). Then he stooped down again to write in the dust.

When her accusers heard this, they slipped away, one by one, starting with the oldest, until only Jesus was left in the middle of the crowd with the woman.

Then Jesus stood up again and saw only the woman. He asked her where her accusers were and if none of them had condemned her. She answered and told him none had.

So Jesus said to her, "Neither do I. Go and sin no more." John 8:11 (NLT).

S tory Analysis

Jesus showed compassion toward the adulterous woman. Truthfully, the Law of Moses required that the woman be stoned, but the law of Jesus is love. Jesus showed love to her and did not allow her to be killed for her sin as the Jewish leaders wanted. The reason Jesus came in the first place was to save mankind from perishing, so he was not going to allow her to be killed when he had come to save her from her sins by dying on the cross.

In his compassion, Jesus made sure he told the woman about her sin truthfully. He did not condemn her, but he told her to stop sinning. Love does not keep a record of wrongs, but it does not cover continued sin. This is because love wants you to be better, so it will tell you when you are wrong. It can be likened to when parents spank their children for doing wrong. It is not because they hate them, but because they want them to be better. While Jesus did not want her to die, he wanted her to be better.

The Jewish leaders had always wanted to test Jesus and see him make a mistake. But Jesus knew their hearts and knew what they wanted him to say, so he always surprised them. They always came to him with one question or the other to trap him, but Jesus knows all and as he was wont to do, used the situation to teach not only the woman, but the judgmental leaders.

$\cdot$ $\cdot$ $\cdot$

𝒯ake-Home Lessons

1. As Christians, we need to show compassion for people who are weak. We should not condemn people because they sin; we should draw them closer and help them be better people. We should not push people away because they are sinners; we should show them love and they will soon see the errors of their ways. Just like Jesus made the Jewish leaders understand that they were not perfect either, as nobody is perfect but God, we also must understand that we are not perfect, so we should be patient when others fall into sin.

2. Compassion does not mean we should cover sin or excuse it. While we should not condemn people and drive them away, we should also not sugarcoat the truth. We should tell people the truth in love and draw them closer, so they can learn to be better. Jesus told the woman to "go and sin no more." That should be our disposition as well when people fall into sin.

3. We should not, as Christians, act like the Jewish leaders, who are always seeking the downfall of another. Instead, our desire should be that people become better. We need to key into the Holy Spirit as Christians so as to always say the right things when enemies are trying to trap us.

𝒬uestions to Contemplate

1. Was Jesus excusing sin when he let the woman go?
2. Why did Jesus stoop down, and what was he writing?

*𝒶*pplication Answers

1. Jesus was not excusing her sin when he told the woman to go, because he also told her not to sin anymore. He does not condemn, but he does acknowledge that a sin has been committed. Jesus is pure and holy and would, therefore, not allow sin to thrive. But he had come to save her from her sins, not push her into destruction. The death sentence by stoning that the Law of Moses stipulated would have been the end for her, and she would have no chance at all to change. But with what Jesus was offering, there was the option of changing and turning away from sin. Jesus does the same for all of us. Have any of us ever died when we do something wrong? No. That is God giving us a second chance to repent and change. The time will come when it will be too late, and there will be no room for repentance. So now, while we have it, let's make use of the opportunity.

2. We do not know why he stooped, nor did the Bible tell us what Jesus wrote when he stooped. But we do know that the first time he did, it showed that he would not speak rashly. He could have answered them immediately, but he took time with his reply. Also, after telling them his judgment, he stooped down again, and that gave the accusers the time to think that they were, indeed, with sin, and so not able to stand in judgment.

Chapter Seven

THE HEALING OF THE SON OF THE WIDOW OF NAIN

Text: Luke 7:11-17

Main Story

Jesus and his disciples went to the village of Nain, and a large crowd followed them. As they were about to enter, they saw a funeral procession coming out of the village gate, for the only son of a widow. A large crowd was following her. Jesus was filled with compassion when he saw her, so he went to her and told her not to cry.

Jesus walked to the coffin and touched it. The bearers stopped when he did. Then Jesus said, "Young man, I tell you, get up." Luke 7:14 (NLT). The dead man sat up and began to talk. And Jesus handed him over to his mother.

Great fear swept among the people when they witnessed that miracle. They praised God and said that a mighty prophet had risen among them, and the news of Jesus spread around the area.

Story Analysis

Jesus was just passing by on his own when he noticed

the funeral procession and discovered it was for a widow and her only son. The widow had already lost her husband, and now her son, who should have served as her companion and confidant, was dead. It was a double tragedy for her, and Jesus recognized this. That is why he was filled with compassion and sought to help her. Jesus was not called to the situation; he offered himself to the situation because he could imagine the depth of her pain. As a widow in that situation, her tears would have been heartrending combined with those of the people following her. Jesus felt it with them and offered to restore her joy, so she would weep no more.

God always rewards compassion. When we show compassion, there is result, because it is coming from a selfless and loving heart. God is love; therefore, whatever proceeds from love is very powerful and able to make changes, even raising the dead. God backed Jesus' act of compassion immediately, and it happened because it was his will. Any time something is done that is God's will, it is done without struggle. All Jesus did was speak to the man; he broke no sweat at all, and the man was resurrected. The mother's delight must have been without measure.

God was glorified. After Jesus displayed the great miracle, drawn from a compassionate heart, it brought glory to God.

Take-Home Lessons

1. As Christians, we should be on the lookout for people we can render help to. They must not come to us seeking help before we can help them. For instance, if we see a blind person or little children trying to cross a busy road, we should always have compassion to help without being called. It is through acts like this that we can show ourselves as Christians who act the way Jesus does.

2. God is always in support of acts of compassion, so he backs

them with his mighty hand. We can rest assured that when we do great things from a heart of compassion, God will reward us with his mighty hand. God will glorify himself because we are doing his will by showing compassion. Selfishness and any act from it will not engender God's backing, but selflessness will see God at work.

*Q*uestions to Contemplate

1. Why did Jesus stop even when he was not called?
2. Jesus touched the coffin of the dead man. Why did Jesus have to touch the coffin?

*A*pplication Answers

1. Jesus stopped because he is compassionate. He thought of how the widow had lost her husband and now her only son. It touched Jesus greatly that the woman would be left all alone in the world and so, even though nobody called him to it, He had to stop and make sure the joy of the woman was restored.
2. The fact that Jesus touched the coffin is significant because, according to custom, a religious leader did not touch a coffin, it was seen as unclean. Jesus was, however, ready to go the extra mile to show that he was with the woman in her pain. He could have easily just spoken words without necessarily touching coffin; after all, this is Jesus we are talking about. But Jesus was ready to strip himself of his elevated position to identify with this poor widow who had just lost her only son. Sometimes, we must flout custom and go the extra mile to identify with people's pain.

Chapter Eight

THE RESURRECTION OF LAZARUS

Text: John 11:1-44

Main Story

There was a man named Lazarus, a brother to Mary and Martha. The family was close to Jesus. This Lazarus was sick, and his sisters sent Jesus a message, telling him about Lazarus's sickness. When the message got to Jesus, Jesus said the sickness was not unto death but for the glory of God. So, although Jesus loved them, he stayed where he was for two more days. Finally, he told his disciples they should head for Judea, but his disciples hesitated because the people of Judea had almost stoned Jesus few days before, but Jesus was not deterred. He told them Lazarus was asleep and he was going to wake him up. His disciples thought he was talking about normal sleep, so they told Jesus Lazarus was soon going to wake up on his own. Jesus had to tell them plainly that Lazarus was dead, and he was glad he was not there, for the sake of the disciples, so they could now believe.

When Jesus got to Bethany, he was told Lazarus had been in the grave for four days. Martha and Mary were home, being consoled by many people. Martha heard Jesus was on the way and ran to meet him. When she got to Jesus, she told him if he had been there, her brother would not have died, but she knew that even now whatever he asked of God, God would do. Jesus assured her that her brother would rise again. He also told her,

"I am the resurrection and the life. Anyone who believes in me will live, even after dying. Everyone who lives in me and believes in me will never ever die." John 11:25-26 (NLT).

When he was done talking to Martha, she went to tell Mary that the master wanted to see her. Immediately when Mary heard, she ran out of the house. The people who were consoling her ran after her, because they thought she wanted to go to the grave to cry. When Mary got to Jesus, she fell at his feet and told him if he had been there, their brother would not have died. When Jesus saw her and others with her crying he was moved. He asked them where they kept Lazarus, then he wept with them.

Jesus followed them to the tomb that they had covered with a stone. He told them to roll the stone aside. But Martha told Jesus Lazarus had been dead for four days already, so it would be unpleasant. Jesus, however, assured her that she would see God's glory if she believed. So, they rolled the stone back and Jesus looked up toward heaven and said, "Father, thank you for hearing me. You always hear me, but I said it out loud for the sake of all these people standing here, so that they will believe you sent me." John 11:41-42 (NLT).

Then Jesus shouted with a loud voice, "Lazarus, come out!" John 11:43 (NLT). And the dead man came out, his hands and feet bound in grave clothes, his face wrapped in a head cloth. Jesus told them to unwrap him and let him go.

S tory Analysis

Jesus knew Lazarus was going to die (or *sleep,* as he called it), but he did not hurry there because, as he told his disciples, he was glad he was not there so that the disciples might believe. Through the death of Lazarus and his ultimate resurrection, Jesus taught his disciples and the other people that he is the resurrection and the life.

Jesus felt the pain of the people, so much so that when he saw them crying, he joined them. This makes us see clearly the humanity of Jesus, that he could be vulnerable even as we are. It also shows us that Jesus is a sympathetic person who feels the pain of others. We see that whenever we are in pain, Jesus is also in pain. He showed it in this story as well as that of the widow of Nain.

Mary and Martha trusted in the compassionate heart of Jesus to come through for them. They knew once he came, the situation would be turned around for good. They were sure that he would feel for them and do something about it. Both of them told him they were sure if he had been there, their brother would not have died, and they were right. But with God, no situation is too late, so even the fact that Lazarus was dead could not deter him.

Take-Home Lessons

1. There are some Christians who are so used to bad things, they do not feel people's pain any longer. That is not the way God wants us to live. He wants us to mourn with those who mourn and rejoice with those who rejoice.

2. As Christians, we should understand that we do not have a high priest who is not touched when things happen to us. He feels sad when we are sad, he mourns when we mourn, he is unhappy when we are unhappy; we should trust in him to come through for us. We should believe in his ability to show up in our case and raise every dead situation back to life, even if it has been dead for four days and smells bad.

Questions to Contemplate

1. Why didn't Jesus go immediately when he was told Lazarus was sick?
2. Why did Jesus cry when the others were crying?

ℐpplication Answers

1. Jesus did not go immediately because he wanted to demonstrate the mighty power of God. The bible emphasizes that Jesus loved Lazarus, but he did not go. This implies that sometimes, God does not do what we want immediately, because he wants to glorify himself through our lives and do even greater things in our lives. We can imagine how Lazarus would have become even more known as the man who was raised from the dead than if he had just been healed of his sickness before he died. It is left to us to be patient with God and see him do wondrous things in our lives. It is not for us to question the motivations of God.

2. Jesus cried because he was moved by their tears. He did not like to see people in pain, and this shows us the humanity of Jesus. Many have argued about Jesus actually coming as flesh, but when we see some of the things he did, we can see that he indeed came as man. He was born, he was hungry, he had friends, he prayed, he ate and he cried—all that we would expect a man to do. So, yes, he knows what it is to be human, and so, feels our pain.

Chapter Nine

THE BLIND BARTIMAEUS

Text Mark 10:46-52

Main Story

Jesus and his disciples were walking with a large crowd at their tail. A blind beggar named Bartimaeus, son of Timaeus, was sitting by the roadside. He heard Jesus was close by, he began to shout, "Jesus, Son of David, have mercy on me!" Mark 10:47 (NLT).

Many people yelled at him to be quiet, but he didn't listen. Instead, he screamed even louder for Jesus to hear him. Luckily for him, Jesus did hear him and stopped. Jesus, then, told the people to tell him to come.

So the people told Bartimaeus to cheer up, because Jesus was calling him. Bartimaeus threw his coat aside and jumped up to meet Jesus. When he got to Jesus, Jesus asked him what he wanted.

Bartimaeus told Jesus he wanted to see. Jesus then said to him, "Go, for your faith has healed you" Mark 10:52 (NLT). Immediately, his sight was restored, and he followed Jesus down the road.

Story Analysis

Jesus heeded the cry of the blind man when others wanted him to be quiet. Others did not think he was important enough to be disturbing Jesus, but with Jesus, every man is important and every man deserves a hearing. Are we like the crowd or like Jesus? Are we shutting people up who need help or are we like Jesus, who stops on his way to help people who need his help. The fact that Jesus stopped does not mean he had no important place to be, but that Jesus would not leave a wounded man unattended to. Ever. That is how selfless he is.

Bartimaeus did not relent in calling on Jesus even when others were trying to shut him up. Let's take a cue from him and cry even more to God when we need his help. The blind man knew he needed help, and that was his last resort, so he ignored the voices of the people telling him to be quiet. As far as he was concerned, Jesus was the one he had dealings with and not the people shushing him. The voices on the street can be loud and intimidating sometimes, and many would have cowered in silence after meeting such opposition, but Bartimaeus was different. He knew what he wanted and was ready to get it. He had faith and was not afraid to shout it out.

Take-Home Lessons

1. Just like Jesus allowed himself to be distracted from his journey to heal a blind man, we also should not be rigid about schedules and our time-table when we see someone in need. We should be flexible enough to be able to adjust our time to help another. We also have the mind of Christ; therefore, we have the ability to be compassionate and selfless, to put the needs of others before our own and make sure they are better off than when we met them.

2. We shouldn't give up easily or listen to voices around telling us God will not listen to us; let us stay focused on him, and his compassionate heart will soon hear us. We can learn a lot from the resilience of blind Bartimaeus, who did not let the voices on the street keep him from reaching for God. We need to understand that our God is a compassionate God, and he is ever ready to help us, so we should not give up till he answers us and grants us our request.

Questions to Contemplate

1. Why did Jesus ask blind Bartimaeus what he wanted?
2. Why was Bartimaeus crying louder when he was told to be quiet?

Application Answers

1. We would wonder why Jesus was asking what Bartimaeus wanted when it was obvious. What is the need of a blind man if not to see? But Jesus knew what he was doing, as always. It could be that Bartimaeus was calling on Jesus because he wanted to greet Jesus, or maybe he needed food. The fact that the problem of people is obvious does not always mean that that is what they want. That is why it is important that we make sure we are prepared for the opportunity we are praying for. There are many people who want God to visit them but when he does, they are not ready to tell Him about what they need and because of that, they miss the opportunity of having answers to their most pressing prayer. If Bartimaeus had mentioned something else, that is what he would have ended up with.

2. Bartimaeus was crying louder because he was determined to get Jesus' attention and get his miracle. It is amazing that even when he was told to be quiet, he shouted even louder. Many would have given in out of fear, or be cowed by the voices of so many, but not Bartimaeus. He was a very relentless and determined man. He was sure of what he wanted, and no matter what people said, he was only concerned about reaching Jesus.

Chapter Ten

THE HEALING AND FORGIVING OF THE PARALYTIC

Text: Mark 2:1-12

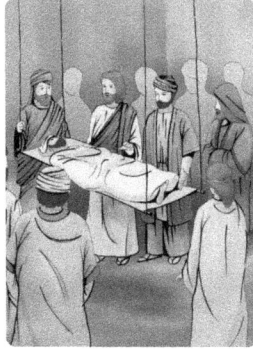

Main Story

Jesus came to Capernaum from Galilee, where he healed many people. He was staying in a house, and a lot of people heard he was there, so they all gathered to see him. They were so many that there was no room in the house or outside. While he was preaching God's word to them, four men arrived, carrying a paralytic man on a mat.

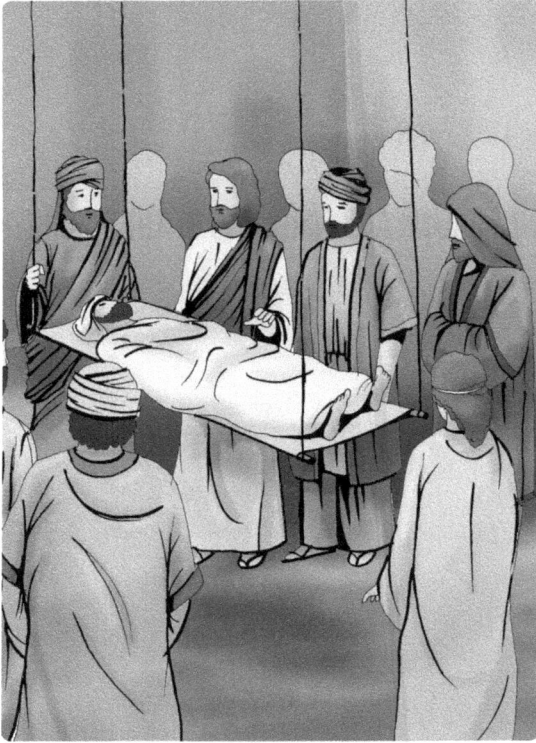

They could not get through the crowd to get to Jesus, so they dug a hole in the roof above Jesus' head. They lowered the man down on his mat, right in front of Jesus. When Jesus saw their faith, he said to the man, "My child, your sins are forgiven." Mark 2:5 (NLT).

Some of the teachers of religious law there thought to themselves that Jesus was blaspheming when he said the sins of the palsy were forgiven, because only God can forgive sins.

Jesus, knowing the thoughts of their hearts, told them, "Why do you question this in your hearts? Is it easier to say to the paralyzed man 'Your sins are forgiven,' or 'Stand up, pick up your mat, and walk'? So I will prove to you that the Son of Man has the authority on earth to forgive sins" Mark 2:8-10 (NLT).

Then he turned to the palsied man and told him to stand up, pick up his mat and go home. Immediately, he leapt to his feet and walked through the stunned onlookers. They were amazed, praising God and admitting that they had never seen anything like that before.

Story Analysis

The friends of the paralytic man were compassionate people. They cared that their friend be healed and they took him all the way to the place where he would find cure. They knew Jesus was the healer and they sought him out. When they got there and the room was full, with their compassionate hearts, they went the extra mile to dig a hole and let him down through the roof. They did not relent at the first obstacle. After all, they could have told themselves they had tried enough and let their friend go at that time. Nobody would fault them for not trying harder to get their friend to see Jesus. But they were not satisfied till they received healing for him, and Jesus was moved by such an act of faith.

Jesus showed compassion by forgiving and healing the man. We as humans err a lot, and if we look at what we do, God has every right to decide not to forgive us. But he does not relate to us on that level. He is so compassionate that he forgives us and does not count our sins against us. Jesus did not leave any stone unturned in healing the man. Despite the Pharisees that were there and ready to count everything Jesus said against him, Jesus was more concerned about healing the man.

Also, Jesus used the opportunity to let the people know that he had been bestowed with power not just to heal, but to forgive sins as well. Jesus was further augmenting his authority over sin, which would ultimately be seen at the cross when he died to save mankind from sin.

Take-Home Lessons

1. How many of us can go the extra mile to help someone? How many of us care enough to go that extra mile? It might not be something we would consider doing, it might be painful or inconvenient, but it is our Christian duty to be compassionate, care about people and go the extra mile to help them. It is our duty to make sure that people feel better. As far as it is in our disposal to help, even if it will cost us something, Jesus expects us to render help. We should not leave people halfway; that is something people in the world might do but, as Christians, we have been called to a higher duty of going the extra mile to help others.

2. We should impart a forgiving spirit and not hold people to a standard. Keeping grudges is not a quality of a Christian; God expects us to let people go and not remain bitter over whatever they do to hurt us. Apart from that, he expects us to render help even in such situations. A Christian cannot turn down a man in need as far as it is in our power to help. Jesus forgave the man of his sins and also healed him. That should be our disposition as well; forgive them and do them good.

Questions to Contemplate

1. Why did Jesus have to forgive the paralytic before healing him?
2. Why did Jesus tell him to take up his mat and walk instead of just praying for him?

*A*pplication Answers

1. We do not know exactly why Jesus forgave the paralytic. It could be because he wanted to show the people he had the authority to forgive sins or because the paralytic's sin contributed to why he was paralyzed. But we do know, from this story, that Jesus has authority over all sins and sicknesses. He can forgive sins and he can heal all sicknesses and diseases.

2. When we read through the healing stories of Jesus, we will see that he used different methods in healing. Some, he prayed for; some, he simply said their faith has made them whole; some, he told to take their mat and walk; and there was even one that he used clay to rub his eyes with. God cannot be limited; he can come to our rescue in any way. All we have to do is trust him. We could also infer that he was testing their faith to believe he had healed him by asking him to get up from that mat through faith. What we need to know is God is at liberty to use any method to save us.

AFTERWORD

Jesus is our standard to follow, and he has given us various examples of living a life of compassion. He *lived* a life of compassion because it was seen in everything that he did. He was always about the people; he was always selfless and sacrificial. Even when it was inconvenient or painful or difficult, when someone needed help, Jesus was there. He expects us all to make his life our example and live the same way. When we do this, only then will we be able to attract people to the goodness of knowing Jesus.

ABOUT THE AUTHOR

James Taiwo is the founder and senior pastor of World Outreach Evangelical Ministry in New York City. He holds a Doctor of Theology degree and a Master of Science Degree in Environmental Engineering. A practicing civil and environmental engineer and preacher, James also plays saxophone and is an avid blogger. With the aim of diversifying the gospel to adapt to the fast-changing technology of our day, he is the publisher of Trumpet Media Ministries and author of several books, including *Bible Application Lessons and Prayers, Book of Prayers, Who Was Jesus Really?, Christian Principle Guides*, and *Roadmap to Success*. James lives in New York City with his wife and children.

CONNECT WITH THE AUTHOR

Please add your honest, positive reviews of this book online.
Rate this book five stars now at
www.bit.ly / pinnacle-compassion-book

Sign up for new book alert from the author at
www.bit.ly / bookalertme

Visit the author's website at
www.jamestaiwo.com

Connect with the author on social media

f facebook.com / jamestaiwoJT

🐦 twitter.com / theJamesTaiwo

a amazon.com / author / jamestaiwo

ALSO BY JAMES TAIWO

Bible Application Lessons and Prayers

Bible Giants of Faith

Christian Principle Guides

Book of Prayers

Who Was Jesus, Really? - Book One

Who Was Jesus, Really? - Book Two

Who Was Jesus, Really? - Book Three

Who Was Jesus, Really? - Boxset

The Pinnacle of Compassion

The Ancient Houses of Egypt

Success Express Lane (Your Roadmap To Personal Achievement)

www.ingramcontent.com/pod-product-compliance
Lightning Source LLC
Chambersburg PA
CBHW071638040426
42452CB00009B/1688